Dinosaur Publications

Going into Hospital

by Althea
illustrated by Maureen Galvani

I would like to thank Professor D. F. N. Harrison, MD, MS,
FRCS of the University of London; Sheila Gatiss and the
National Association for the Welfare of Children in Hospital;
and Addenbrooke's Hospital Cambridge, for their advice
in the preparation of this book.

Published by Dinosaur Publications Ltd Over Cambridge England

ISBN 85122/069/X   Copyright © Althea Braithwaite 1974

In hospital you sleep in a large room
with lots of other children.
It is called a ward.

Hospitals smell different from home.
Lots of the beds have sides like cots,
so if you are feeling ill
you can't fall out.

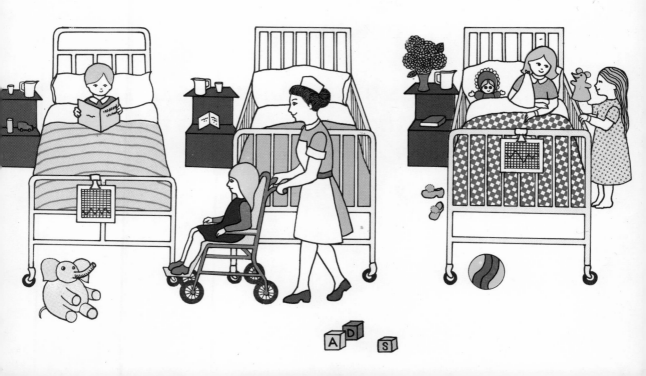

You have your own cupboard
by your bed to keep
your toys and things in.

Sometimes the hospital has a bed
for your Mummy to sleep in too.
But if she can't stay
she will try to come
and visit you.

There are lots of
other children in the ward,
so you soon make friends.

Let's see what some
of the children
in this ward are doing.

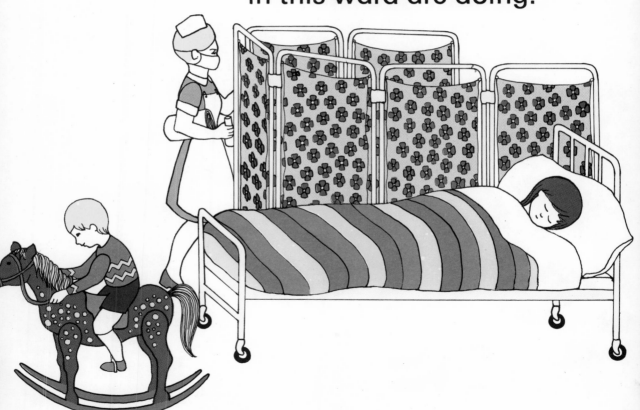

Everyone is having lunch.
Can you see what it is today?
After lunch the teacher
will come to help some of the
children with their lessons.

Lisa isn't well enough
to eat, so she is having
special food which is liquid.

It is put into her arm
through a tube which is
a bit like a straw.

John broke his leg
falling out of a tree.
He has a special hard plaster
on his leg to keep it straight
while it is mending.

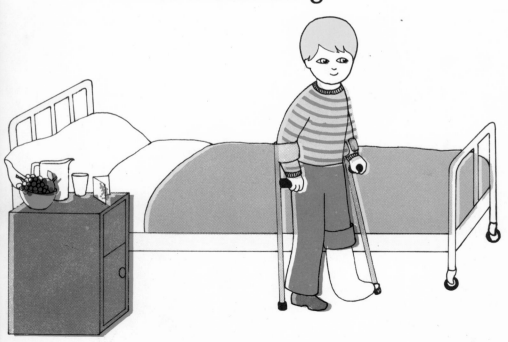

The lady in the white coat
is pricking Anne's finger.
She squeezes out a
little drop of blood,
so she can test it.
Anne says "ouch!"

Ben came to hospital
in an ambulance !
He had a very bad pain
in his tummy.

He has had an operation
to make him better, but he
will still feel sore for a bit.

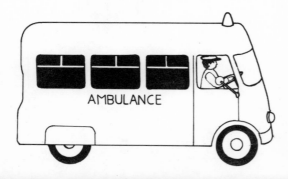

He doesn't want to get up today. So when he wants to go to the toilet the nurse will bring him a special potty.

Sharon is going to have
an operation too.
She gets a sore throat
lots of times in the winter.

She has come into hospital
to have her tonsils out,
so her throat will be better.

The nurse gives Sharon
an injection to make her feel sleepy.
It makes Sharon's mouth
feel a bit dry too.

Later Sharon is wheeled
on a trolley up in the lift
to the operating theatre.

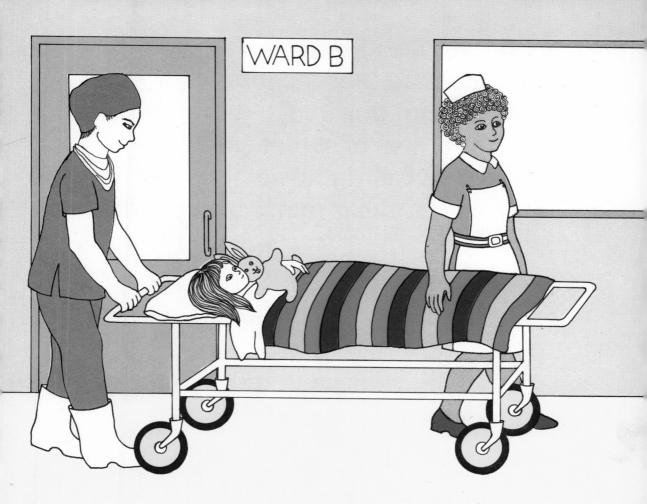

The doctor gives Sharon
a black mask to breathe into.
It has a special gas in it
which has a sort of sweet smell.
It makes a whistling noise
when you breathe into it.

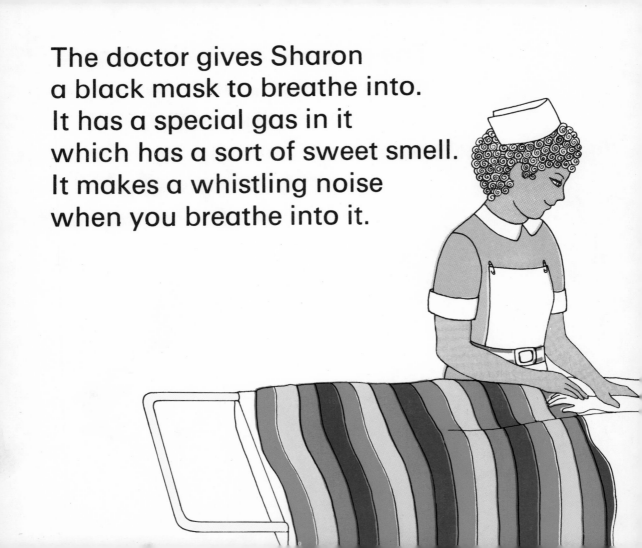

The gas will make Sharon
go fast asleep, so that
she doesn't know anything
about her operation.

When Sharon wakes up
she is back in her own bed !
She feels a bit sick
and her throat hurts a lot.

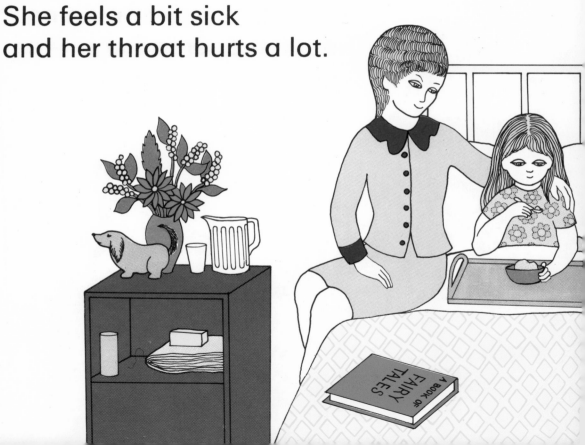

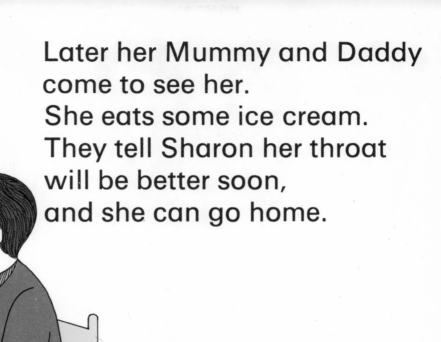

Later her Mummy and Daddy
come to see her.
She eats some ice cream.
They tell Sharon her throat
will be better soon,
and she can go home.

The hospital doctor comes each day
to see how all the children
are getting on. Sometimes he brings
other men and ladies with him.
Some are learning to be doctors.